Coyote Ridge Elementary School
13770 Broadlands Drive
Broomfield, CO  80020
720-872-5780

## DATE DUE

|  |  |  |  |
|---|---|---|---|
|  |  |  |  |
|  |  |  |  |
|  |  |  |  |
|  |  |  |  |
|  |  |  |  |
|  |  |  |  |
|  |  |  |  |
|  |  |  |  |
|  |  |  |  |
|  |  |  |  |
|  |  |  |  |
|  |  |  |  |
|  |  |  |  |
|  |  |  |  |
|  |  |  |  |
|  |  |  |  |

Demco, Inc. 38-293

*Communities at Work*™

# Community Spirit

## *Symbols of Citizenship in Communities*

**Angela Catalano**

The Rosen Publishing Group's
**PowerKids Press**™
New York

*For Mom and Dad for the past thirty-four years.*
*And for Frank, for the next thirty-four years—and beyond!*

Published in 2005 by The Rosen Publishing Group, Inc.
29 East 21st Street, New York, NY 10010

First Edition

Editor: Natashya Wilson
Book Design: Maria E. Melendez
Layout Design: Albert B. Hanner

Photo Credits: Cover and pp. 1, 5 © Associated Press/AmesTribune; p. 7 © Alan Schein Photography/Corbis; p. 9 © Reuters NewsMedia Inc./Corbis; p. 11 © Peter Beck/Corbis; pp. 13, 19, 21 © Associated Press; p. 15 © Reuters NewsMedia Inc./Corbis; p. 17 © Reuters NewsMedia Inc./Corbis.

Library of Congress Cataloging-in-Publication Data

Catalano, Angela.
Community spirit : symbols of citizenship in communities / Angela Catalano.
    v. cm. — (Communities at work)
Includes bibliographical references and index.
Contents: Symbols of citizenship — Community symbols — Community spirit — Fairs — National holidays — The American community — The American flag — The national anthem — The Declaration of Independence — A proud community.
ISBN 1-4042-2784-9 (lib. bdg.) — ISBN 1-4042-5020-4 (pbk.)
1. Citizenship—United States—Juvenile literature. 2. Patriotism—United States—Juvenile literature. 3. Community life—United States—Juvenile literature. [1. Citizenship. 2. Community life.] I. Title. II. Series.

JK1759.C37 2005
323.6'5'0973—dc22

2003025338

Manufactured in the United States of America

# Contents

# Symbols of Citizenship

A **community** is a place where people live or meet often. There are **rural**, **suburban**, and **urban** communities. A country, such as the United States, is also a community.

**Citizenship** is being part of a community. Good citizens take care of their **responsibilities**. Voting, following laws, and learning about community **symbols** are important responsibilities.

*Voting has become a symbol of American citizenship. It is an important responsibility. Here citizens who are 18 years old and older line up to vote for community leaders.* ▷

# Community Symbols

Many things can be community symbols. Your school may have a symbol, such as an animal, that stands for the school.

Colors can be community symbols, too. For example, the red, yellow, or green color of a stoplight is a symbol. These colors tell people to stop, to be careful, or to go.

*Stoplights are symbols that help citizens to follow laws about safe driving. When the stoplight is red, drivers know that they must stop their car and wait their turn.*

# Community Spirit

Community symbols can raise citizens' community spirit. Having community spirit means being proud of the community.

Citizens may show community spirit by beautifying the community for a holiday. They may take part in a parade or cheer for other citizens who are marching in it.

*These high school students show that they are proud to be part of their school community by wearing the school's colors.*

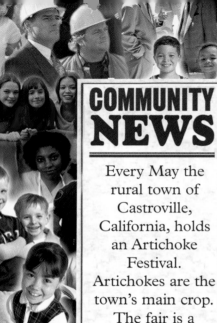

## Fairs

Some communities hold fairs that have become symbols of those communities. Citizens show their community spirit by taking part in the fair. These fairs bring the community together. Fairs allow people to share their pride in something special about a community, such as an apple harvest or an important event.

*This girl has won first prize for the sheep she has raised. Fairs allow people to take pride in themselves and in their community.*

# National Holidays

The United States has many national holidays. They include New Year's Day, Martin Luther King Jr. Day, **Memorial** Day, **Independence** Day, and Labor Day. Americans show their American community spirit by learning about these holidays. Americans also show their spirit by sharing these holidays with friends, family, and other people in the community.

*Many American communities have parades on Independence Day. Citizens show their American spirit by flying the American flag. Many people wear red, white, and blue, which are the colors of the flag.*

# The American Community

The United States has many symbols that bring American citizens together as one big community. The bald eagle is America's national bird. It is a symbol of power and freedom.

The **Pledge** of **Allegiance** is an important spoken American symbol. A person who says the pledge is promising to be a good American citizen.

*Some schools begin each day by having students and teachers say the Pledge of Allegiance.*

15

There are many rules about how the American flag should be flown. One rule is that the American flag should never touch anything under it, such as the ground.

# The American Flag

The American flag is a symbol of American citizenship. It has 13 stripes of red and white. The white stands for goodness. The red stands for bravery. The flag also has 50 white stars on a blue rectangle. The stars stand for the 50 states. The blue stands for **justice**, or fairness.

*Many Americans fly the American flag outside of their houses to show their American community spirit. Schools and government buildings fly the flag, too.*

# The National Anthem

The national anthem, or song, of the United States is called "The Star-Spangled Banner." It is another symbol of American citizenship.

Francis Scott Key wrote the words to the anthem in 1814. He was writing about seeing the flag while he was locked up on a British ship during a war. The sight of the flag gave him hope.

*The national anthem is played and sung at the beginning of many events. People take off their hats and place their right hands over their hearts when they hear the anthem.*

Thomas Jefferson wrote the declaration. Benjamin Franklin and John Adams helped Jefferson. American leaders agreed upon the declaration on July 4, 1776.

# The Declaration of Independence

The **Declaration** of Independence is another important symbol of American community spirit. When the declaration was written, America was ruled by Great Britain. The words of the declaration said that Americans wanted to be independent. It helped Americans to form the United States of America.

*After the declaration was written, 200 copies were printed on July 4, 1776. Only 25 of the those first 200 copies are still around today. Here children take a look at one of the copies.* ▷

# Proud Communities

Community spirit is important to communities of all sizes. Learning about community symbols is an important part of belonging to a community.

Good citizenship also means **participating** in a community. For example, you can show your school spirit by paying attention in class. When citizens have community spirit, they help their community to succeed.

# Glossary

**allegiance** (uh-LEE-jents)  Support of a country, group, or cause.

**citizenship** (SIH-tih-zen-ship)  Being a member of a group.

**community** (kuh-MYOO-nih-tee)  A place where people live and work together, or the people who make up such a place.

**declaration** (deh-kluh-RAY-shun)  An act that makes something known.

**independence** (in-dih-PEN-dents)  Freedom from the control of other people.

**justice** (JUS-tis)  Fairness.

**memorial** (meh-MOR-ee-ul)  Something used to remember a person, a place, or an event.

**participating** (par-TIH-suh-payt-ing)  Taking part in something.

**pledge** (PLEJ)  A promise or agreement.

**responsibilities** (rih-spon-sih-BIH-lih-teez)  Duties that a person must take care of or complete.

**rural** (RUR-rul)  In the country or in a farming area.

**suburban** (suh-BER-bun)  Having to do with an area of homes and businesses that is near a large city.

**symbols** (SIM-bulz)  Objects or pictures that stand for other things.

**urban** (UR-bun)  Having to do with a city.

# Index

# Web Sites

Due to the changing nature of Internet links, PowerKids Press has developed an online list of Web sites related to the subject of this book. This site is updated regularly. Please use this link to access the list:

www.powerkidslinks.com/caw/comspirit/